BUTTERFLY INFLUENCE

Paxton Darrell Grayer II

Copyright © 2020 Paxton Darrell Grayer II

All rights reserved

The characters and events portrayed in this book are fictitious. Any similarity to real persons, living or dead, is coincidental and not intended by the author.

No part of this book may be reproduced, or stored in a retrieval system, or transmitted in any form or by any means, electronic, mechanical, photocopying, recording, or otherwise, without express written permission of the publisher.

Paperback ISBN-13: 9798663046039

Cover design by: Creative Krew LLC
Library of Congress Control Number: 2018675309
Printed in the United States of America

This book is dedicated to all of those seeking a friend in their plights. For those who are confused about who they are, or where they are going.
Thank you to my grandmother Irene Arellano Davis (5/9/1951--10/13/2019) whose last words to me were, "have purpose." To my mother Misty Michelle Arellano, my brother Anthony Pierson, and four sisters Aarika, Brianna, Adrianna, and Deseray.
My four uncles: Bobby, Michael, Jaime, and Marshall Davis Jr. My three aunts: Monica Arellano (4/17/1973--5/3/2016), Nina, and Pricilla Davis. And all those connected to me by blood and spirit.

And to my wife, LeAndra Rose Grayer, thank you. To my son, Agod Divine Sol Grayer, be the light.

CONTENTS

Title Page	1
Copyright	2
Dedication	3
Foreword	7
Chapter 1: The Egg	8
Chapter 2: The Caterpillar	10
Chapter 3: The Pupa	13
Chapter 4: The Butterfly	16
Chapter 5: Change Is the Only Constant	18
Chapter 6: Different Clans Still Friends	20
The law of love	23
References	24

FOREWORD

Everything with a breath knows what it it to suffer. Some suffering is self-caused, while other forms of suffering are out of our control. All can agree upon that. So how does one have patience during times of suffering? How does one get out of suffering? What is the cause of suffering?

> My journey from darkness to
> light inspired this work.

During those dark times, I would imagine myself as a caterpillar on his way to becoming a butterfly, knowing change was coming, and that I would soon be out of the hell I was in, as long as I focused my energy on doing so.

> Energy flows where our thoughts go.

A caterpillar is born and dies; a butterfly resurrects from its juices (Krulwich). The beginning and end. The end and the beginning. This work entails the human life journey explained through the life cycle of butterflies. The goal of this literary work is to raise self-awareness in the hopes of promoting self-healing through inner realization.

CHAPTER 1: THE EGG

Butterflies go through four stages of growth in their life cycles: egg, caterpillar, chrysalis, and adulthood.

Stage 1

Three to six days after the female has mated, she seeks out the perfect plant to lay her eggs. The mother spends a great deal of time checking plants to ensure they are the right species for egg-laying. She tastes the plants to determine the level of toxicity. The plant must be chemically correct or else the larva could die.

The leaf is the foundation for the larva's growth.

Childhood as the foundation for our growth

Everyone has parents according to the flesh. Some have spiritual parents. Others adopt through law. It is obvious, Parents are of high importance. Knowledge of ourselves comes through our parents or guardians.

Childhood is the foundation for our growth. It is the start of the molding process via personality, thought patterns, and habits. We only know what we consume. What our guardians allowed us to record with the eye of our mind, and what we have consumed on our own free will.

Where there are guardians offering warmth and nourishment, there also are secure, emotionally balanced children. Where there are distant guardians, there also are insecure, emotionally imbalanced children.

The patterns of our Guardians have a significant impact on the patterns of our future.

Meditation: What was childhood like for you? What type of environment are you creating for your child/children?

CHAPTER 2: THE CATERPILLAR

<u>*Stage 2*</u>

Once hatched, all the caterpillar knows is consume. It eats half if not the whole leaf it hatched on. It then travels through the world, using natural DNA instincts to guide it toward the right leaves for nourishment. Whether the larva thrives for 2-6 weeks or becomes food for another species, this stage does not last long.

However, it is the most important stage.
If the larva does not eat enough or is malnourished, then it will not complete metamorphosis.

<u>*Discovery Mode*</u>

Let us substitute the word eating with discovering. From the moment one is born and even until death, they are discovering so much about themselves and the world or eating everything around them. At a youthful age, we are taught virtues and vices or good and evil. People told us that having virtues or practicing them will ensure a bliss life. As infants, we roamed around the house putting items in our mouth. If you have ever held one, then you know the struggle of keeping your finger out of their mouth. Infants just want to eat everything. We hear the words, "that's bad for you" and "that's good for you," as we go about in our stage of discovery.

At the core, we are trying to figure out
what we are, who we are, and why we are.

As previously mentioned, this is the most important stage for both the larva and us. This is when our Life Circle forms. The Life Circle holds what we believe, what we know, and what we value.

What we believe finds what we know, and
what we know decides what we value.

What happens in the second stage is based on what occurs in the first stage. We are who we are based on the type of environment our parents hatched us in, what various people told us about their experience in the first stage, and what we tell ourselves in our minds.

One thing we all have is free-will. This we will use for eternity because we are energy. And energy is neither created nor destroyed. **It only changes forms.**

Can we learn to redirect and control this energy for the benefit of ourselves and those around us?

Where there are healthy, nourished rich foods, there also will be healthy nourished thoughts.

Where there are unhealthy, spoiled foods, there also will be unhealthy, spoiled thoughts.

We only know what we eat.

<u>Meditation</u>: In every adult, lies a little child. That inner child controls the adult.
Are there any unresolved issues from your past that are interfering with your now, your current state of living?

CHAPTER 3: THE PUPA

Stage 3

Now that the larva has eaten enough food, it can begin the 3rd stage, pupation, or metamorphosis. This can take 1-40 weeks depending on the species. Meaning travel at your pace because it is your race in this game of life. You vs. you. A wise gentleman once said, "I'm not competing with anyone. To compete with an individual means they have something I want, and nobody has anything I want. I am content with room left to grow."

Remember, in the first stage, the larva traveled through grassy terrain looking for food in the sunlight. Now it must enter the darkness. After attaching itself to a leaf or stem, the caterpillar covers itself with silk or its skin hardens into a shell forming a chrysalis. Though it appears cut off from the world, it is in fact in tune with the uni-verse or the one verse sung by the source of All.
What is the meaning of entering the darkness? It is both literal and metaphorical. What happens when

you close your eyes? Is not darkness present; however, one can create light from within.

<u>*You, too, have a chrysalis*</u>

Just as the larva entered into itself, we too must go inside ourselves to the source of All changes and work from the inside out and bring it to the light field or where things are made manifest. Meditation is the way for doing this and it comes in many forms; however, isolation is important.

Your temple or body, mind, and
soul is your chrysalis.

Everything starts with a thought. Our parents thought and spoke about us before we were here. Thoughts live at the center of darkness in one's mind. They travel faster than light. Our thoughts are images created by the source of All within us.

What is the foundation of a thought? Thoughts come from what we intake not only at birth but on a continuous basis. Thoughts are memories from our past, giving life to the now, which is simultaneously giving birth to the future. Everything starts with a thought. Thoughts are the foundation for All things existing. However, some thoughts are not our own. We cannot help who our parents are, or what environment we are born into. Eventually, we must learn to control our thoughts generating from our own temple.

Forgiveness is of high importance in this stage. As we look at ourselves via past, present, and future, through the eye of our inner mind, we must see a being who was in discovery mode, attempting to balance out their truths and lies.

<u>Meditation</u>: How can one master the voice or thoughts in their mind, if they are afraid to be alone with the voice, or do not know how to do so since everything starts with a thought?

Those who learn the inner voice, and how to control their thoughts will morph into a butterfly. Remember, not all larva become butterflies, meaning not everyone will reach this stage, instead pass on patterns to their children that create the same cycles instilled in them.

CHAPTER 4: THE BUTTERFLY

Stage 4

Butterflies spend most of the time trying to find a mate in the final stage, so the cycle can repeat itself all over again for their descendants.

The cycle of life.

The butterfly, no longer a caterpillar, given brand-new organs, has died unto itself. Two different creatures. The butterfly could not go back to its old ways if it wanted to. Through wisdom, they realize the only way to do that is to procreate and seek to add to the foundation taught by their guardians to ensure the survival of their species.

We, too, search for mates

It is obvious that butterflies do not go about seeking to find a caterpillar to mate with. Instead, they find another butterfly. One suitable for their new body. One that will uplift them. One they can be themselves around.

If it were to find itself around a caterpillar than it **risks** the chances of completing its purpose for coming into existence.

<u>Meditation</u>: Are your current relationships a reflection of who you want to be?

CHAPTER 5: CHANGE IS THE ONLY CONSTANT

Change starts with YOU or Your Own Universe. Take a moment and observe your soundings. Take a 30-second break from reading, take slow deep breaths, and just see.

What did you see? Notice everything around slowly changing. The couch, air, weather, your child/children if you have any, and you yourself. Everything is constantly changing for the better or worse. That depends upon the being whom the change is emitting from.

> An ancient maxim, "you can only control yourself." So, take control today.

The butterfly no longer acts like a caterpillar meaning your old-self cannot go where your new-self is. Put off the old and clothe yourself with the new. Put off guilt, shame, insecurities, and all that prevents you from becoming the butterfly you were meant to be.

Figure 1:   -9 -8 -7 -6 -5 -4 -3 -2 -1- 0 1 2 3 4 5 6 7 8 9

Look at the numbers above in figure 1. Each day each of us starts at 0. A positive plus a positive equal a positive. Each positive choice one makes builds upon another, as it is negative. Each thought of discouragement breeds more discouragement. Either you are building or destroying yourself and or your family. The irony of figure 1 is we move from left to right throughout seasons in our lives, often finding ourselves back at 0. One could attribute it to both micro and macro aspects of your life. The light and dark are forever at work coexisting with one another. Find a balance between the two.

Knowing that change is the only constant, let us harness the energy of change, and make it a friend.

CHAPTER 6: DIFFERENT CLANS STILL FRIENDS

Ants and butterflies display both parasitic and mutualistic relationships, depending on the type of species. Our next discussion will take us to Europe where the Adonis Blue Polyommatus bellargus butterfly and Myrmica sabuleti ant are indigenous. They share a mutualistic relationship. Unlike the Butterfly cycle mentioned in chapters 1-4, this cycle holds a detour into another species layer.

Adonis Blue females lay their eggs on short plants. This creates a shorter distance of travel that is more convenient for both the larva and ants. "The ants protect the larvae from predators and parasitoids, and even bury the larvae (in groups of up to eight) in loose earth cells at night. The Adonis Blue overwinters in the larval stage and pupates in the upper soil surface, often within ant nests where pupae continue to be attended by ants until the adults emerge" (Martin and Wigglesworth).

Why do Ants protect them? It is because of honey-like secretion from the glands and pores of the larva, that is "milked" out by the ants. Milking can go on for as long as 9 months or until metamorphosis. In addition, the larva "sings" for the ants, or generates a vibratory sound that resembles that of their Queen, which makes it soothing for the ants, and prevents the ants from eating it.

<u>We all need somebody to lean on</u>

Whether help comes from another species such as a dog, universal factors such as rain and sunlight, or another human being, **we are all depending upon something or somebody.** It goes against nature to be alone for lengthy periods; however, creating moments of isolation for self-reflection via meditation helps one's body, mind, and soul.

For me personally, help came from various sources. Like Adonis Blue, I was able to live with another family different from my own, in which we both received help from each other greatly. Learned and still am learning how to be a dad from other successful dads not related by blood, but by spirit. During the time I was in a cocoon, I too had ants standing around in protection over me, that came in the form of **true agape like** love and friendship.

Through trust and forgiveness from others and myself, I went from a caterpillar to a butterfly.

THE LAW OF LOVE

To love your neighbor as yourself is
to love the creator because we are all
made in the image of the creator.

REFERENCES

Krulwich, Robert. *Are Butterflies Two Different Animals in One? The Death And Resurrection Theory*. 1 Aug. 2012, www.npr.org/sections/krulwich/2012/08/01/157718428/are-butterflies-two-different-animals-in-one-the-death-and-resurrection-theory.

Warren, Martin, and Tom Wigglesworth. "Adonis Blue Polyommatus Bellargus". *Natgeos.Com*, 2020, https://natgeos.com/wp-content/uploads/2018/12/adonis_blue-psf.pdf. Accessed 23 June 2020.

www.learnaboutbutterflies.com

Made in the USA
Middletown, DE
07 January 2023